MW01037268

BROKEN VESSELS:

GOD'S POWER THROUGH AUTISM

BY: DEBORAH DENNIS

Dedication

To my husband, Greg - thank you for loving and supporting me through thick and thin. After twenty years, you're still my hero.

To my son, Gregory – I'm so proud of you. You make me believe that I didn't do such a bad job after all.

To my son, Devin – I love your adventurous spirit. Never let anyone but God decide who you are. Not even me.

To my youngest son, Owen – Baby, you're the reason why I wrote this book. I'm so thankful God gave you to me.

TABLE OF CONTENTS

Chapter One: Something is Wrong 11

Chapter Two: Getting Diagnosed 17

Chapter Three: Here Comes the Anger 25

Chapter Four: A New Dream for Owen 31

Chapter Five: Leaving and Going Back 37

Chapter Six: Broken Vessels 43

Chapter Seven: Me, Broken 47

Chapter Eight: Revelation 51

Chapter Nine :   Children of the Called 57

Chapter Ten: Finally, an Answer 63

INTRODUCTION

For the ones who choose to read this book, please understand that I am not claiming to be an expert on Autism. I am simply the mother of a beautiful, unique child with Autism, whom I love with a viciousness. I am also the daughter of a Heavenly Father who loves me in the same manner, and loves Owen more than I could ever imagine. In Him is my hope, my being, my son's healing. I choose to believe that "in all things God works for the good of those who love Him, who have been called according to His purpose."

I pray that this book brings a little more understanding to the ones suffering with Autism, and a renewed faith in our Sovereign God who sees all, knows all, and can heal all.

Habakkuk 2:2
Then the Lord replied:
"Write down the revelation and make it plain on tablets so that whoever reads it may run with it."

CHAPTER ONE

Something is Wrong

Owen Beau Dennis was born on July 25, 2005 at 8:13 a.m. in the morning, weighing 9lbs. 1oz. The third son born to my husband Greg and me, he was a beautiful child from the start, screaming loudly because the doctor had dared to pull him from his place of solitude. I had no idea the many times Owen would have to be pulled from that place.

He seemed like a typical baby. I remember the nurses talking about how healthy he was. "We can tell you ate healthy, Mrs. Dennis." As he grew, I began to get the feeling that he was going to be special. Granted, every mother feels that way about her child, but I do believe that God was preparing me, even then, for what Owen and I would face.

As a baby, he had his quirks, not as eager to engage with my husband and me as his two brothers before him. Loud sounds seemed to bother him more than most babies, and even then, it was hard to get his attention. I particularly remember one morning when Owen was still an infant, that I was having a hard time calming him. At that moment, God placed in my heart that he was special, and I would have to stay calm in order for Owen to stay calm through all circumstances. Now, that was hard for me, being a "high-strung" person, always wearing my emotions on my face. Even then, God was teaching me to trust in Him not only for me, but on the behalf of my young, fragile son. Yet, through it all, I loved this "quirky" baby, and just assumed that everything would be just fine.

I can't remember his exact age when I realized that something wasn't quite right. But I did notice that he didn't seem to be hitting those developmental milestones like other babies. In our church, I was pregnant with about three other women. While their babies were pulling up, walking, saying their first words, squealing when they saw their mothers, Owen, while sweet, was lagging behind. I remember telling myself, "He'll catch up," but the gap was getting bigger and now there was this small voice in the back of my mind, whispering "Something is wrong."

But how could that be? I am a God-fearing mother who prayed over my unborn child every day. I ate healthy, didn't smoke or drink, took vitamins and every precaution that a good mother is supposed to take. But that small voice kept whispering.

When Owen started to show an unusual fascination with strings and strands of hair, the voice kept whispering. When I would find shoes lined up going down our hallway, like children had stepped out of them and kept walking, the voice started getting louder. I noticed how he would flap his hands like a bird, or instead of playing with a toy, he would run circles around it, laughing. That voice was now screaming at me, every odd behavior throwing up a red flag in my mind. And Owen still was not talking. On top of everything else, he had started making odd faces while wringing his hands, for no apparent reason. Plus, there was still the problem of getting even the briefest eye contact with him.

As I had always done my entire life when faced with situations that I could not fix, I went to God. "Lord, what is wrong with my son?" After much prayer, the Lord answered, "He has Autism." My first response was complete shock, then numbness. Was I being punished? After all, I'm far from perfect. If that was the case, then why was my son suffering? I assure you that I struggled with the "sins of the mother" debate with God for a while, with no immediate answer from Him. I'm ashamed to say this, but for a few months, I just acted like I didn't hear that from God. When the thought of my beautiful son having Autism would enter my mind, I would just bury it under other things and try my best to handle the issues at hand.

Yet, the issues at hand were getting bigger. It seemed as if with each passing day, Owen was falling further behind. Along with the odd behavior, not playing with toys appropriately, he was not eating well. As a baby, he would gag at times when I would feed him formula, and subsequently some of it would come up. I thought at first he had reflux, but when that was ruled out, on the advice of the doctor, we switched his formula to something more easily digested. I had hoped he would like baby food better (God knows it had to taste better than formula!) Wrong. He tolerated it at best. So as soon as he turned a year, I started supplementing his diet just to make sure he was getting the nutrients he needed.

Not to mention that he was having problems sleeping. It was hard to get him to settle down at night, and then once asleep, he would wake up every 3 or 4 hours. Greg and I were taking turns getting up with Owen just so that we could function during the day. With sleep deprivation added to all the concerns that we had for our son, we were wearing down. Quickly.

The biggest problem still seemed to be Owen not communicating with us. He had started to say a few words, here and there. I will never forget the first time he said "mommy" and with eye contact! Owen was a little over 2 ½ years old. It was Easter Sunday and he had crawled up in my lap and just looked at me saying, "mommy, mommy." I sat there, warm tears rolling down my face, thankful for the moment, but knowing I had to do something, fight for Owen, if necessary. I had no idea that day how hard I would have to fight.

CHAPTER TWO

Getting Diagnosed

When I took Owen to his pediatrician for his 2 year check-up, I expressed my concern to the doctor about him not talking. The doctor, at that time, didn't seem to be concerned about it. He told me about "third child syndrome" (they have a name for everything now!) in which the youngest child will be delayed in talking because he has older siblings to talk for him. I had also talked to the doctor about the fact that Owen had not started walking until 16 months. (We would laugh at him, he had about 4 different crawls! The wounded soldier crawl, the prairie dog crawl...). We used to joke that Owen wouldn't walk because he would keep reinventing the crawl, therefore there was no need. By 16 months, though, it was no longer cute, it was alarming. But all the doctor would say was, "Let's wait and give him more time, we'll talk more at his 3 year check-up." I found out later that this "wait and see" approach is very common with doctors when dealing with children later diagnosed with Autism.

I left the doctor's office knowing that it was time for me to take matters into my own hands. My second son had chronic ear infections as a baby that delayed his speech development. When I had taken Devin, then 2 years old, to see an Ear, Nose and Throat Specialist, very quickly they discovered he wasn't speaking because he couldn't hear! Two sets of tubes, adenoids and tonsils removed, fixed that problem. When Devin could hear, he quickly began to speak and hasn't stopped talking since. So the only thing I knew to do was to take Owen to that same doctor and have his hearing checked. I scheduled an appointment for March 20, 2008.

Boy, that was a visit not soon forgotten. The doctor's examination of Owen's ears showed everything was intact physically, with no fluid or abnormalities, but the poor doctor suffered several kicks (to tender areas) by a shrieking Owen, all the time with me practically sitting on my toddler just to get through the examination. By the grace and mercy of God, the audiologist just happened to be in the office that day, and Owen (me, too) was put in the sound room to try to check his hearing. We got through that test okay, I guess. I think I was already too traumatized by the physical exam to remember much. Afterwards, we were put back in the exam room to wait for the doctor to get the results.

When he walked back in, I knew something was wrong (besides him being sore from Owen's attack). He told me that Owen had no hearing problems, but he felt that we needed to go to Children's Healthcare. I looked at him and asked him, "Doctor, do you think my son has Autism?" He looked at me and said, "It's a very good possibility." I asked him, "Would you have told me that if I had not asked?" He answered, "I would have had to." I remember going back into the waiting room with Owen while they set up the appointment, feeling overwhelmed. I decided to get on the phone with my husband, Greg. You see, I had not told him what God had said months before. So, I got on the phone, told him what the doctor had said, and finally what God had told me. They other end was quiet for a moment, and then Greg told me,

"Deborah, I know. I just didn't know how to say it to you." Apparently, the only ones we were kidding were ourselves, in keeping this from one another.

I knew something had to be done quickly. With each day, it seemed another problem was emerging. Owen had started to hit and bite out of frustration. I'll never forget the first time he bit me. I was in the kitchen, trying to catch up on some cleaning, when he started crying. I got eye level with him, asking him, "Son, what's wrong? I wish you would talk to me." The next thing I knew, Owen is biting my arm. Hard. I jerked back in surprise, not quite knowing what to do. I looked at him standing there, with tears streaming down his face, frustration written all over it, and asked God, "What do I do?" At that moment, I happened to look at the clock, and realized that time had gotten away from me, and that Owen was probably hungry. I can't remember what I gave him to eat, but it was obvious that's what he wanted. Still shaken by the incident, I knew that God had to move for Owen and give me the wisdom to know what to do.

On March 27, 2008, Greg and I took Owen to Children's Healthcare of Atlanta for a Speech Evaluation. We were put in a playroom with toys that a "typical" child would have found interesting. Not Owen. He was much more concerned about being in a new place and staying put in my lap. In came a young woman, who identified herself as a speech therapist. For an hour, she tried to engage Owen in play, identifying objects and making eye contact with her. It was painful to watch. Sitting there, I realized just how much my son needed help. At the end of the visit, she told us that Owen had a "severe receptive/expressive language disorder" and needed to see a developmental pediatrician. She also talked to me about how sign language could "bridge the gap" and provide a way of communicating with Owen. Well, I jumped on that with both feet. She showed me a few signs, like "more," "please," and "all done." I remember practicing them all the way home.

I don't know what was more frustrating, being told over and over that something was wrong with my son, or being sent to another doctor for an "official diagnosis". I couldn't make anyone come out and say the word "autism." The developmental pediatrician would have to do that. An appointment was set up for us to go and see one in Atlanta, but it wasn't until May 21. Meanwhile, the only thing I knew to do was to practice signing with Owen, and work on the few ideas that the speech therapist gave me.

I thought that May 21 would never come. So once again, Greg and I packed up Owen and drove to Atlanta to see yet another doctor. Once there, they put us in a hospital-looking room, and left us there. For the next four hours, teams of people came in and out, observing Owen and asking questions. I had brought with me copies of doctor's notes, the hearing test, and the speech evaluation with me. I had made up my mind that SOMEONE was going to tell me exactly what was going on with my son and what we needed to do about it. In the midst of all that, every once in a while, the developmental pediatrician would pop in to see how we were doing. At one point, I turned to Greg and said, "You know how the obstetrician will monitor a woman in labor, let the nurses do the majority of the work, then at the last moment come in and catch the baby? How much you wanna bet that's what this doctor is going to do?" Sure enough, when everyone else had their say, the developmental pediatrician came in to "catch the baby." He sat down, looked at us, and said, "Owen has Pervasive Developmental Disorder, Not Otherwise Specified." We looked at him, and I asked, "What does that mean?" He explained to us that it was on the Autism Spectrum, somewhere between Mild Autism and Asberger's Syndrome. He also assured us that with therapy, Owen would be able to function in society, but we had our work cut out for us for the next few years. Finally, someone had said it! I left there, physically and emotionally exhausted. Owen seemed to handle the experience better than I did. On the ride home, I felt so overwhelmed. We didn't have insurance. We owned our own business, and had a mediocre health insurance policy. But as soon as I called them to see how much they would cover for all the evaluations, they quickly told me that they didn't cover any of that. I remember demanding them to tell me why, only to be told, "You should have bought a policy with more coverage." We were already strug-gling to pay for that coverage, let alone pay more. So after much discussion, we dropped the policy and decided to pay for the visits with the money we were spending on apparently useless insurance pre-miums. What I didn't realize was how much money it was going to take to get Owen the help he needed, let alone to pay for all the evaluations. Once again, I turned to the only One who could help us. "God, please help us. Make a way for us to get Owen the help he needs."

CHAPTER THREE

HERE COMES THE ANGER

In the midst of all this, we were still going to the same church. Greg and I both knew that people had already come to the conclusion that there was something "wrong" with our son, we could just feel it. It was very hard. The one place we should have been lifted up in prayer and supported, we felt like we were not. It's almost like everyone took a few steps back from us, with a death grip on their children, mind you. I remember telling one mother, "My son is not contagious! If that was the case, every kid in daycare would have Autism!" Looking back on it, I probably judged them too harshly, they just didn't know what to say or do. There is still so little known about Autism, I had only vaguely heard of it myself.

As a family, we were all dealing with Owen's diagnosis in our own way. Greg became increasingly more protective of Owen, but for the most part, didn't want to talk about it. Not to me. Not to our family. Especially not to church people. My oldest son, Gregory, wasn't handling it much better. While able to talk to a few close friends about it, he had also become very protective. I remember him coming home one day from school, upset because he had "snapped" and pushed another teenage boy against the wall for bullying a fellow classmate who had Autism. My middle son, Devin, started to deal with feelings of anxiety about Owen's safety (he still does to this day) and the responsibility of "fixing" his little brother. I was informed of this through a meeting with his teacher at school. Feeling overwhelmed, Devin had confided in her and she had brought in the school counselor and me to talk about it. We were all feeling the pain of Owen's diagnosis.

But I seemed to deal with it the worst. Although God was moving for Owen in a mighty way, I was becoming increasingly angry. Owen had been approved to go to a Special Needs Preschool in the fall. Because of his diagnosis, he had been approved for health coverage through the state of Georgia, that would cover all of his medical needs. This included the speech and occupational therapy that he would need to have twice a week. He was even going to get additional speech therapy through the preschool once he started. I was told over and over, "You must be Super Mom! I have never seen a child diagnosed so fast, and get help so fast!" To which I would reply, "No way, God has given me favor." All the while, I was angry. I was angry that my son was suffering with something so terrible, and seemingly....final. I was angry at the church for not being more supportive. I was angry at God. After all, I had tried so hard to be a good Christian, praying with people at the altar at church, ministering to the youth on Wednesday nights. And this is what I get?! Looking back, I'm amazed and thankful that God didn't hold Owen accountable for my attitude. In spite of me, God was still moving for Owen.

I remember one afternoon in particular. I had just gotten off the phone with our Youth Pastor. I told him I wasn't coming to church. When he asked why, I told him that I couldn't stand to walk by all the other church people who I didn't think tried nearly as hard as I did, and yet had healthy children. I know that is a terrible thing to say or feel. I looked over the fact that God had given me two sons before Owen who were healthy. And it's not that I wanted anyone to have children with Autism. I wouldn't wish that on any child. Anger is such an irrational emotion. No matter how you stack the facts against it, there it is. I remember stomping inside, hot tears stinging my face, feeling angry, hurt and betrayed. As I stepped into the living room, I heard the TV. Greg called out to me, "Deborah, you got to see this." Choosing not to respond, I stomped into the kitchen, but I could still hear the television.

Greg was sitting there watching an interview on a Christian channel with a man who was born with no arms or legs. He was talking to his interviewer about his disabilities, the goodness of God, and all the people he had been able to minister to. The interviewer wanted to know why the man thought he had been born with such a disability. As I stood there, I heard the man tell the story of Jesus and His disciples in John Chapter 9. If it doesn't ring a bell, let me remind you. Jesus and His disciples come across a man blind from birth. The disciples asked Jesus, "Rabbi, who has sinned, this man or his parents, that he was born blind?" To which Jesus replied, "Neither this man nor his parents sinned, but this happened so that the Glory of God might be displayed in his life."

The paraplegic man went on to say that if he had been born with arms and legs, he would not have been able to witness for Jesus to as many people. "You see," he explained, "everyone is willing to listen to anything a man with no arms or legs has to say. Because of this, I have witnessed to people all over the world for the Glory of God." Then my Father whispered to me, "For My Glory. It's not your fault. This is for My Glory." God is so good. Even now as I write this, the tears fall. I realized that my "broken" son was being chosen for the Glory of God.

I wish that I could say that all the anger melted away in that moment, but it didn't. I grieved for a year after Owen was diagnosed. I grieved for him, and what could have been. If you have a child, you will understand what I'm about to say. When you hold your baby in your arms for the first time, dreams are born. What is he going to be? A football player? A doctor? A musician? Will he get married some day? Will he have children of his own? I felt like I was holding shattered dreams for my son in my hands, and all I could do was weep over them. There were many days that I threw myself into the daily activities of taking care of my family, taking Owen to therapy, studying over the sign language book I had gotten from a speech therapist that God had brought into our lives, just to fall apart in private. I know what it is to feel emotional pain so intense that it feels physical. But through this time, God sustained me. He strengthened me, and let me know that He not only was aware of Owen, but had everything under control.

CHAPTER FOUR

A NEW DREAM FOR OWEN

It was now the Spring of 2009. Even with all of my fear and anxiety over Owen starting Preschool (I was so afraid of him being mistreated, and because of his inability to talk, he wouldn't be able to tell me), he had handled the transition fine and was making progress. He had also started private speech and occupational therapy and it was looking hopeful.

Even with all of the good things happening, I was still grieving. I don't know why, but I grieved until May 21, 2009. The first year anniversary of Owen's diagnosis. When that day came, it was like I took a deep breath, said "Okay, we're doing this" and I was done. As hard as that time was, I'm sure it was a necessary process.

But before then, I had attended revival at our church in April. The minister who was preaching was young, energetic, and a prophet. He had been to our church a few times before and was notorious for prophesying to people in the middle of his sermons. I had gone that Sunday morning without Greg or Gregory because they were working at our new house that we were building.

I wasn't "on top of my game" that morning, because I had a terrible dream the night before. I dreamed that Greg and I were in the sanctuary of our church, and we were rummaging through a closet looking for basketballs for the youth to play with. I stepped out of the closet to see a very large snake. This snake would make an anaconda look small. Worst yet, it was swallowing Owen. Greg started to fight the snake, but all I could do was wring my hands and cry, feeling completely hopeless. That dream

upsets me to this day. I woke up in a cold sweat, ter-
rified. I knew as soon as I woke up, that the snake in
the dream was Autism, and I felt that Owen wasn't
even safe in the sanctuary of the House of God. I
remember praying until I fell back asleep, because a
spirit of fear had overwhelmed me to the point that I
felt like I couldn't even breathe.

By the time I got to church, all I wanted to do was
slide down in my seat and somehow get some spiritual strength. I remember listening to the choir sing
during the worship service, and remembering the
dream, I said in my heart, "Lord, make a way where
there seems to be no way." Then the Lord answered
me, "Not only will Owen speak, he will sing and
many will be blessed." Immediately I saw Owen in
my mind, singing on the stage in our sanctuary, with
a microphone in his hand. Once again, all I could do
was cry. It's funny, I never considered myself a crier,
but that seems like all I had done since Owen was
diagnosed.

Thankful for His promise, I sat in my seat
thinking God was finished with me. Wrong again.
By this time, the prophet had started preaching. I
don't even remember what he was preaching about,
I was still thinking about what God had said. Until I
noticed him standing over me, reaching for my hand.
I had seen him do this several times, taking someone
by the hand, still preaching, until God gave him the
words to say. He started up center aisle with me, and
about the time he got to the front, he said, "I feel
the Holy Ghost." Then he started prophesying to me,
"What you thought was dead, just reach out your

hand!" The power of God fell, and the next thing I knew, I was on the floor.

God revealed to me that everything that appeared hopeless or "dead" in my life was going to require faith in Him to be revived again. Psalm 126: 5-6 says:

"Those who sow in tears will reap with songs of joy. He who goes out weeping, carrying seed to sow, will return with songs of joy, carrying sheaves with him."

You see, God permits us to grieve as long as we believe in Him as we sow seeds of Faith. Psalms tells us that our tears water the seeds we carry, causing a harvest in our lives. The very thing that we weep over, when we carry it to God in faith, He breathes life into what we thought was dead.

That day, God asked me to trust Him with the dead seed of Hope that I was carrying in my hand. "Weep over it, water it with your tears. Then plant your seed in My Word, and believe me for a harvest of Healing," His Spirit whispered to me.

My son will be healed from Autism.

CHAPTER FIVE

LEAVING AND GOING BACK

It's amazing to me how God interlaced all of these promises in the midst of my anger, fear and frustration. In spite of the condition of my heart, God had promised a new dream for Owen to replace the ones I felt that he had lost to Autism, plus confirmation from a prophet!

But the last year had taken a physical toll. The rest of my family seemed to be doing better, Greg was finding it easier to express how he felt about Owen's condition, and my two other sons had adjusted as well as anyone could expect. At that time, I had stepped down from the Youth Department in our church, feeling that I needed to give my full attention to my family. But a few months later, after feeling that I needed to go back, a disagreement occurred within the department and I was asked to step down from the position I held. Once again, feeling rejected and hurt, I left the church and the rest of my family followed.

For six months, we were away from the church. During that time, I swore I would never go back, to that church or any church for that matter. I never stopped loving God, I just didn't particularly like His people. (Anybody else been there?) I felt I had given everything, and then when I was down, all they could do was kick me and my family instead of praying for us.

As angry as I was during this time, God was still speaking, still promising, still good. I never understood how much God loved me until then. I knew He had not wanted us to leave the church. He had sent us there in the fall of 2004, and had not told us to leave.

In that six months, God dealt with me, showing me that my focus had been all wrong. After all, I had wanted the approval of people too much, and was looking to them to meet my needs instead of looking to Him.

We left the church in June 2009, and after a few months, we were all feeling less hurt. In spite of that, I justified not having to go back. It's funny how God always knows how to change our minds.

Having a heart for Special Needs children, I had decided to be a substitute teacher in the county that we live in. I was hoping to have a positive impact, and truthfully, I was trying to find a way to minister to people without doing it within the church walls. Look, there's nothing wrong with that. In fact, Jesus commissioned us to go out into the world, but my heart was wrong. Bottom line, it doesn't matter what others do to us, we stand before God alone and must account for ourselves only.

So, there I was, joking with a sheriff at the police department in our county, because (thankfully!) a criminal background check is required to work with children in the school system. I had nothing to worry about. I had never committed a crime, I had only had one speeding ticket in my whole life! But within a few days, the sheriff's office was calling me to tell me that my prints came back with a rap sheet a mile long. Needless to say, I was stunned! I couldn't believe that this was happening to me!

"Don't worry, Mrs. Dennis," they told me, "we can tell by looking at you that you are not a criminal. It's obviously a mistake. Come back up here and we will redo the prints." So back up there I went, shaken, but feeling sure that it would be cleared up quickly. Wrong again. Within days, I'm receiving the phone call from the sheriff's office that the same results happened with the second set of prints. It seems that someone else's criminal background was now tied to me. The only thing that was saving me was that the other woman was older than me and apparently started her life of crime while I was in middle school. I know by now you are thinking that I'm making all this up, and I wish I was.

Extremely upset, I asked the officer, "What am I supposed to do?" "Mrs. Dennis, you need to contact Florida, that's where her first arrest was made." And then he said, no lie, "Look on the bright side, at least she doesn't have any warrants out for her arrest!" I couldn't believe it, this sounded like a movie script, not something happening to me. I remember calling my sister about it, only for her to laugh for five minutes before she realized that I was not joking.

It took about a month to clear my name. Every time I would cry out to God, the only thing He would say was, "Who are you?" And I would answer, "Lord, you know I'm not perfect but I didn't do this. I can tell you who I'm not." And then I would start my long list of things that I was not guilty of. Kind of like the pious Pharisee praying aloud by the sinner in the parable of Jesus, now that I think of it.

Finally, God moved, and after going to the Georgia Crime Lab in Decatur, Georgia with Greg, being reprinted and having the FBI do a national search to clear my name, it was over. I tell you, I have never been so scared than when I went to that crime lab. I remember my knees shaking and then bursting into tears when the officer told me that my name was clear. I made sure that I got documentation before I left, I meant not to repeat that experience ever again! It still sits in my safe. Just in case.

It was October 2009 now, and once again, I found myself trying to catch my breath from the latest continuous drama in my life. A few days after my name was cleared, I remember talking to the Lord, thanking Him for moving for me. Once again, He asked, "Who are you?" By this time, I knew all my answers and excuses were not holding up. Then humbly, I answered, "I am your servant," and knew that was the right answer. Then God said, "Consecrate yourself. Be holy, for I Am Holy. Then go back."

I knew right away God was calling me back to the church that I had left feeling hurt and rejected. This time, I knew that it would be different because I was different. I told Greg what God told me. "Why do we have to go back? Why didn't God speak to me instead of you?" he asked. I told him, "I asked God the same question. He told me that He told you in 2004 to take our family there and that He never told us to leave. I pulled us away." Still, for several months, we discussed it, and honestly, dragged our feet in doing what God told us to do. Even though I knew God had done a tremendous work on my heart, I was unsure if I was strong enough to handle another round of church life. So once again, God gave me a dream to seal the deal.

CHAPTER SIX

BROKEN VESSELS

In the dream, I was in a church (not ours) and the minister was giving an altar call at the end of his sermon. As I had seen many times in many churches, the minister was practically pleading with God's people. "If you want God to move in your life, in your family, if you want a fresh move of God, you need to come to this altar," he said.

I was praying at the front of the church, and I saw some people come and kneel down at the altar. Strangely, there was a white chalk line running down the middle of the altar area, and people would bow down to pray, falling forward right up to that chalk line, but never passing it. At that moment, God spoke to me and said, "Everyone wants to have a fresh move of God, but no one wants to be broken. You can't pour new wine into old wineskins. Your breaking began when Owen was diagnosed with Autism."

In the dream, I remember falling on my face and over that chalk line, crying. I thought about that dream for a long time. Jesus had told the Pharisees the very same thing when they were questioning his method of doing things. You can't pour new wine into old wineskins. If you do, the new wine will burst the skins, the wine will run out, and the wineskins will be ruined. (Luke 5:37)

It's human nature to want God to move for us, as long as it doesn't cost us too much, or it doesn't cause too much discomfort. There may as well be a chalk line at the Altar of God, because our attitudes say, "God, I'm willing to yield to Your will (if You move for me) but only to a certain point. I'm not willing to cross this line." Truly that "chalk line" is the point where we completely give up control of our lives, and finally, let God have His way.

If we want a fresh move of God, new anointing on our lives, we must be broken and allow God to remake us and renew us, in His image. We cannot hold the anointing (wine) within our vessels (wine-skins) as long as we have our old way of thinking and doing things. If God poured new anointing into us in this state, we couldn't contain it. Only when we become pliable clay in the hands of God, can He truly fulfill His will in our lives. Only then, can we see a real move of God in our families, our church, our communities, and in our country.

Up until God showed me this, I thought Owen was broken. Owen isn't broken, he needs a healing. But I sure needed to be broken. I had become so resistant, that I was useless in the hands of God. After all, I had my own ideas about the way things should be handled. I had forgotten that I was just the creation, not the Creator. The time had come for me to be obedient once more, and to allow God to fight my battles.

So I consecrated myself, which in Webster's terms means to "declare something to be holy; to dedicate to sacred uses"[1]. I had to get rid of my anger, and my wrong attitude toward the people who hurt me, and allow God to clean my heart.

CHAPTER SEVEN

ME, BROKEN

So, just a week before Christmas 2009, we went back to our home church. Because God had done such a work in me, I knew that I could hold my head up high, knowing His love for me, and that I was a work in progress. Surprisingly, I remember several people welcoming us back, expressing how much they missed us. We got through the next few Sundays just fine, trying to be obedient to what God had instructed us to do. Little did I know, I was headed for another God Encounter.

It was Sunday, January 10, 2010. I remember feeling emotionally overwhelmed that previous week. I thought maybe I needed to recoup after the holidays, and that was it. I remember having a nagging, continuous pain in my right hip that week. When it started, I remember thinking, "great, another ache," and just chalked it up to getting older.

So, there I was that Sunday, headed to church with my family, thinking I was going to go through the motions, I certainly didn't have the energy for anything else. Greg and I had a terrible fight the night before (one of those silly fights that seemed important at the time) and I had told him that I wanted a divorce. "I'm doing the best I can, I can't take anymore! Nothing seems to be good enough!" I told him. Luckily, he didn't take me seriously. But I was most certainly at the end of my rope in every area of my life, just about to let go. Funny, that's exactly where God wanted me to be, where He wants all of us to be. If God can tell the Apostle Paul, "My grace is sufficient for you, for My strength is made perfect in weakness," then it was surely good enough for me.

Even so, there we were headed to church, pretending everything was fine for the sake of the kids, when a minister came over the radio talking about how Jacob wrestled with God. Only when God broke Jacob, particularly in his hip, could Jacob (Deceiver) be renamed Israel (One who had power with God). I listened, tears rolling down my face, wondering about my own sore hip, and what God could possibly want to do with me, only to get to church and the guest minister preached on the same thing! I knew God was speaking to me, so when the altar call was given, I was one of the first ones up.

By this time, in such emotional pain, I told God (and meant it), "Lord, do something in me, or kill me!" When my knees hit the altar, I broke. I remember praying louder and harder than I had in a long time, and it didn't matter to me who heard. I knew that I had come to a crossroads in my life, and I was either going to let God completely have His way, or continue down the self-destructive path I was on. I knew my only hope was in Him.

So I let go of everything that Sunday morning, no longer having the strength to carry it all. I remember at one point in the midst of my praying, I saw a huge hand with tiny pieces of clay in the palm. I knew right away that this was the hand of the Almighty God, my Redeemer, my Creator, my Strong Tower, and those insignificant clay pieces were me. It had been six months to the day since I had left the church, and I had finally allowed God to break me.

CHAPTER EIGHT

REVELATION

I remember getting up from the altar feeling clean and vulnerable all at the same time. I knew that if God had gone through so much trouble to break me, surely something wonderful was going to come of it all.

The next couple of weeks passed without incident, I had a renewed zeal for a close relationship with God, and had started spending personal time with Him through studying, prayer and meditation. I had come to the conclusion that if God never did anything about my circumstances, never healed Owen, it would not change who He is. I had come to the place where I could trust Him like never before, therefore I didn't have to fret about what He chose to do or not do, in my life. I think when we come to that place, where we trust His heart, not His hand, we "free" God to move in supernatural ways.

Amos 3:3 tells us, "Do two walk together unless they have agreed to do so?" When we stop pulling on the hand of God, urging Him to walk faster, slower, or in a different direction, and just simply trust Him as we walk with Him, then God can move in our lives, uninhibited by our will.

Because I was finally in the place to truly trust and listen to Him, God finally spoke to me about Autism. It was Sunday January 24, 2010, and we were in service at our church. It had been a good service, but not a particularly unusual one. Pastor had called for everyone who would, to come to the altar for a few minutes to pray at the end of his sermon. So there I was, praying to myself, thanking God for all the things that He had done in my life. Just about the time everything seemed to be winding down, I heard the pastor say, "Where's Deborah Dennis?" I opened my eyes, a little startled, he had never called for me during altar service. When I looked around, I saw Pastor motioning to me while saying, "I want you to come and pray for this young woman. She has a son with the same diagnosis as Owen. Her son has Autism."

That was all I needed to hear. I went to the other side of the altar and saw a young woman kneeling, cradling a wiggling little boy and praying. I remember thinking, "This scene looks familiar," knowing I had done the exact same thing with Owen. As I kneeled down to pray with her, the power of God fell, and the next thing I know, we were both in the floor.

God ministered through me to her, and when He was finished, I fell into a heap on the floor wailing, "Not another, God! He can't have another child!" That coming out of my mouth was a complete surprise to me. I had never even considered blaming Satan for Autism. I knew the Enemy got a kick out of children suffering, but I didn't think he was necessarily to blame.

I had blamed myself, God, the environment, vaccinations, putting Owen's bottles in the microwave, and so on, for Autism. I can't tell you the number of conversations I've had with teachers, doctors, friends and family where the possible reasons for Autism were discussed. "What do you think is going on? A few years ago, no one had even heard of Autism. Now, one in a hundred children is being diagnosed, with boys four times more likely to have it. What is going on?" That's usually the opening for every discussion I have ever had about it. Up until this point, I speculated just like everyone else.

Now brace yourselves. I'm about to say something totally revolutionary and to some people without spiritual ears, absurd. After I had gotten up from the altar and hugged the mother and child I had prayed with, I heard the voice of Almighty God. He said:

"He has said, I will shut the mouths of their children with Autism." Once again, I stood there stunned, not knowing what to think. I immediately knew that the "he" that God had spoken of, was Satan. I remember walking over to my pastor and his wife, telling them what God had just said, begging them to pray with me.

In between sobs, I told my pastor, "I know what she (the mother I prayed with) is going through. I know the unbelievable pain that families go through when they have a child with Autism. I have tried to reach out to them, but it's like they cocoon themselves in the pain and rejection that Autism brings, and I can't reach them. Why aren't they in church? Where are they? This is where they need to be!"

I remember my pastor listening and telling me, "I know how hard this has been on you, but this may be the reason why God has allowed you to go through this." Then they both prayed with me for God to birth ministry in me, to reach out to families not only dealing with Autism, but all Special Needs. I left there feeling that God was about to do something awesome, but I still needed a little more understanding about what God had said.

CHAPTER NINE

CHILDREN OF THE CALLED

So, after spending time with God, this is what He explained to me:

Satan has launched a strategic military attack on children, particularly on the sons, but not excluding the daughters, of the called. He is doing this to counter-attack the fulfillment of Joel 2:28, a promise which was later prophesied again by Peter in Acts 2:17-18, after the Holy Ghost made His arrival on Earth on the Day of Pentecost.

What does that mean? Simply, if you have a child with Autism, you are called of God. You may not realize it, you may not even have a personal relationship with God at this time, but it doesn't change the fact that God has His hand on your life, with a purpose in mind. You are marked by God for a special purpose and Satan sees it, even if you don't. Knowing what's coming, Satan has launched an attack on your child. Let's review just what Joel 2:28-29 says:

"And afterward, I will pour out my Spirit on all people. Your sons and daughters will prophesy, your old men will dream dreams, your young men will see visions. Even on my servants, both men and women, I will pour out my Spirit in those days. "

I think it is obvious that we are living in the last days. Most scholars will tell you that there are no biblical prophesies left to fulfill before Jesus comes again as He promised. Even if you are a little skeptical of prophesies, just look around. I think everyone can agree that the world, morally, economically, and even environmentally, is in the worst shape it has ever been in. Even nonbelievers can agree that we are headed for even more trouble if we don't change.

Take heart. As bad as things are, our troubles require precious little effort in the hands of God.

This world is in the mess that it is in, because as a whole, humanity is walking in disobedience to God. So God has left us to our own devices. What have God's people always done when they get in trouble? We come to our senses and call on God. This is nothing new. This scenario is played over and over again throughout Bible History. God's people turn away from Him. God leaves them to their own ruin. When circumstances get unbearable, His people cry and call on Him. Then God requires them to change their way of thinking, which changes their actions, and their hearts turn to Him again. Then God moves, heals, blesses His people once more. Only for a generation or so later, the cycle to begin again.

People are crying out, searching for something, like never before. They need something, but really don't know what. The answer to our troubles has always been the same answer. God. Satan knows that it is only a matter of time before God's people remember Him and call on Him once more. And don't forget that God had promised a great outpouring of His Spirit in these last days. Hell was designed by God for Satan and his demons, not for us. The outpouring of His Spirit is to reach every possible person who will turn to Him and be saved before Judgment Day.

Look back at Joel 2:28: "Your sons and daughters will prophesy." In an effort to quench the outpouring that is coming, Satan attacks with Autism. Let's face it, they can't prophesy of the goodness of God, if they can't speak at all. I know that this sounds outrageous, but I know the voice of God. I know what He said.

I truly believe that the only way I could receive this revelation was to have Autism attack my child, my heart. I also believe that this type of revelation will be received better if told by someone who is experiencing the same attack. I'm ashamed to say this, but until I had a child diagnosed with Autism, I never gave one second of thought to all the families that suffer with this everyday. After I got over the shock of Owen being diagnosed, I remember begging God to forgive me for being so self-centered. Isn't that the way we are, though? We don't care about other people's sufferings nearly as much as we should. Not until suffering knocks on our door. Then we get frantic, wanting something to be done. I can say this because I was guilty in the first degree.

So, now that we know Autism is a spiritual attack, what do we do?

CHAPTER TEN

FINALLY, AN ANSWER

I think to find the answer to the spiritual attack called "Autism," we need to go back to the Word of God. Let's look at the scriptures leading up to the promise of Joel 2:28:

Joel 2:12 -14 says:
"Even now," declares the Lord, "return to me with all your heart, with fasting and weeping and mourning. Rend your heart and not your garments. Return to the Lord your God, for He is gracious and compassionate, slow to anger and abounding in love, and He relents from sending calamity. Who knows? He may turn and have pity and leave behind a blessing – grain offerings and drink offerings for the Lord your God."

God, once again, is calling for us to return to Him with a repentant heart, reassuring us of His goodness. Let's look at Joel 2:15-17:

"Blow the trumpet in Zion, declare a holy fast, call a sacred assembly. Gather the people, consecrate the assembly; bring together the elders, gather the children, those nursing at the breast. Let the bridegroom leave his room and the bride her chamber. Let the priests, who minister before the Lord, weep between the temple porch and the altar. Let them say, "Spare your people, O Lord. Do not make your inheritance an object of scorn, a byword among the nations. Why should they say among the peoples, "Where is their God?"

Now more than ever, we need to "sound the alarm," not just on Autism, but on every attack of Satan. We have allowed the enemy of our soul to deceive us. Sounding the alarm will rouse us and everyone around us, from the "spiritual sleep" we are in.

1. Declare a holy fast. I know fasting is not popular anymore. But it is so necessary. I once heard a minister say that Fasting and Prayer are the spiritual power twins. There is something about denying your flesh of what it wants. It always gets the attention of God. It did in the Bible, it will now.

2. Call a sacred assembly and gather everyone, including the children. I'm not saying the answer to Autism is to get back in church. Believe me, I know the problems and short-comings of the church. It's much more than that. "The church" was never meant to be just the place we go to worship. WE are the church. We are the temple. When we con-secrate ourselves, i.e., clean up our hearts and make it a holy place for God's spirit to dwell in once more, we are to assemble our-selves together in worship, which just hap-pens to be in church. But even more than this, God is calling His people to reach out to one another again. I truly believe one of the biggest weapons Satan uses against us, is keeping us so busy to the point that we don't have time for anyone in our lives, beyond the

people that we live with. Think about it. Fifty years ago, we didn't have near the technology that we have today. Has it made our lives easier? In a lot of ways, yes. (Believe me, I take advantage of every gadget that I can to make my life easier as the mom of three children). But we are busier now more than ever. I remember hearing stories of people gathering on front porches in the evenings with friends and neighbors, just talking with each other, while their children played in the streets. Not anymore. My family moved into a little neighborhood a few years ago, and you would never know that children even lived there. I think we can thank video games for a lot of that. Not that we adults are any better. We are so bogged down with everything that we think is important, that we have neglected to build and keep relationships with one another. Then we text message, and blog on our computers, thinking that we have stayed connected. Having 300 friends on the Internet is not the same as human contact. This generation has bought into the biggest lie that Satan has told us. There is no substitution for having personal relationships with each other. It's time that we start "gathering" again. In the Bible, when people gathered in the upper room in "one mind, one accord," the power of the Holy Ghost came. There is power when we stand together. Satan is doing everything imaginable in this day and age to keep that from happening.

3. Then we are to cry out to God to remember us once again. God called for our ministers to "weep between the temple porch and the altar," the place where the people are assembled, and cry out to God to remember us. Not only do we need to have a right heart before God, so do our ministers. Weeping between the temple porch and altar puts our spiritual leaders in a position to feel the hearts of their people once more, and enables them to petition God with more understanding. Ministers were never meant to be put on pedestals. Their job is to do exactly what this scripture says; to stand with, and intercede for, the people.

4. Because of the disobedience of God's people, we have become a "byword, an object of scorn" among other nations. Other nations and religions have laughed at us and made fun of us. When we lost our relationship with God, we lost our power with God, leaving them to say, "Where is their God?" I remember hearing stories as a young girl about the power of God in the Church, and it's time for those stories of long ago to become our reality of today.

Finally, Joel 2:18 says, "Then the Lord will be jealous for His land and take pity on His people." For the next ten scriptures leading up to the Spiritual Outpouring of Joel 2:28, God promises to heal our lands, drive out our enemies, repay us for the years of suffering.

I know that this may seem a lot to process. But if we want our children healed from Autism, our churches healed from indifference and agendas, our homes healed from strife, and our nation healed from moral decay, poverty, disease and every evil under the sun, there is only one thing we can do.

Sound the alarm. Fellow brothers and sisters in Christ, blow the trumpet. It's time for the Church to BE the Church God intended it to be. Join me in fasting and prayer for healing. When we unite before God, consecrated vessels, crying out to Him, He will do just what His Word promises.

I know the day-to-day toll that Autism takes on its victims, and their families. Even as I write, Owen is still getting speech and occupational therapy, still struggling with daily activities that typical children do automatically. I've done what God has required of me through His Word for Owen to be healed. Yet, I still wait for the grasp of Autism to be broken.

I started this book with a verse from the book of Habakkuk. I have written down the revelation and made it as plain as I could. You have read it, now run with the promise. Just know what the following scripture says:

Habakkuk 2:3 says:
"For the revelation awaits an appointed time; it speaks of the end and will not prove false. Though it linger, wait for it; it will certainly come and will not delay."

My son's healing has an appointed time. His healing may be the beginning, or it could be right along with everyone else with Autism. What's beautiful about God's promises, is that we don't have the capacity or power to make them come true. If we did, why would we need Him?

Until then, I will hold to the promises of God, and if needed, I will weep over the seed of Hope until healing comes. Not just for my child, but every child with Autism. A harvest of healing is coming, God's word says so.

Notes

Chapter Six: Broken Vessels

1. Webster's Pocket Dictionary and Thesaurus, copyright 2005, V. Nichols

CPSIA information can be obtained
at www.ICGtesting.com
Printed in the USA
BVHW040241270523
664938BV00005B/290